MEMORY'S DAUGHTER

Memory's Daughter

ALICE MAJOR

THE UNIVERSITY OF ALBERTA PRESS

Published by
The University of Alberta Press
Ring House 2
Edmonton, Alberta, Canada T6G 2E1

Copyright © 2010 Alice Major

LIBRARY AND ARCHIVES CANADA CATALOGUING IN PUBLICATION

Major, Alice
     Memory's daughter / Alice Major.
(CuRRents)
Poems.
ISBN 978-0-88864-539-5
     I. Title. II. Series: Currents (Edmonton, Alta.)
PS8576.A515M44 2010   C811'.54   C2009-906596-7

All rights reserved.
First edition, first printing, 2010.
Printed and bound in Canada by Houghton Boston Printers, Saskatoon, Saskatchewan.

A volume in (cuRRents), a Canadian literature series.
Jonathan Hart, series editor.

No part of this publication may be produced, stored in a retrieval system, or transmitted in any forms or by any means, electronic, mechanical, photocopying, recording, or otherwise, without the prior written consent of the copyright owner or a licence from The Canadian Copyright Licensing Agency (Access Copyright). For an Access Copyright licence, visit www.accesscopyright.ca or call toll free: 1-800-893-5777.

The University of Alberta Press is committed to protecting our natural environment. As part of our efforts, this book is printed on Enviro Paper: it contains 100% post-consumer recycled fibres and is acid- and chlorine-free.

The University of Alberta Press gratefully acknowledges the support received for its publishing program from The Canada Council for the Arts. The University of Alberta Press also gratefully acknowledges the financial support of the Government of Canada through the Book Publishing Industry Development Program (BPIDP) and from the Alberta Foundation for the Arts for its publishing activities.

for Bill and Mary

Contents

    Baucis and Philemon 1

EVE LEARNS ENDEARMENTS
    Eve learns endearments 5
    Eve's children 9
    Eve waters the garden 12
    Eve raises her hand to the tree 15
    Fall in the garden 17
    Eve sings lullabies 19
    Eve studies botany 20
    World spelled backwards 21

MEMORY'S DAUGHTER
    Glosa: Memory's daughter 25
    Vastly out of scale 27
    Time scale 28
    Princesses and frog 29
    Deep field experiment 30
    The gorgon's head 31
    Penelope weaving 32
    Glosa: Parting 33
    Suncatcher 35
    What I will need to hold your ashes 36

AND WE ARE HERE
    Here 39
    Retort as furnace 40
        The Industrial Revolution 40
        Come to nature 42
        Vienna exposition, 1873 43
    Orphanage as machine 44
        Solution to a problem of production 44
        Moving parts 46
        Force fed 48
        For the children 49

Gas light 50
    The gas mantle I 50
    The dangers you can live with 51
    My mother as history 52
    The gas mantle II 53

The Movies 54
    Persistence of vision 54
    Oh, Rose Marie, I love you 55
    Maytime 57
    Song 59

Transport 60
    Romance 60
    Camouflage 62
    Book passage 63

Clocks 65
    The uniformity system 65
    Escapement 66
    Assembly line 67

Explosives 69
    Hell's kitchens 69
    The Ballad of Red Clydeside 72
    The Tory Candidate comes to call 74
    Red Mary 75

Camera 76
    Latent image 76
    The studio photographs 78
    The accidental snapshot 79
    Diagnostic imaging 80

Lullaby for my mother 82

TIME IS HOW

Time is how 85
Lines that break apart 86
The fish is not a plant 87
One thing becomes another 88
Enjambment 89
The million generations 90
The radiant array of plumages 91

Time, infinitely patient, joins 92
Have not the power to recant 93
Begins to breed 94
One cell that senses light grows into eye 95
I am not bird nor ever could be 96
Feather emerges from scale 97
The generations that encage 98

METAMORPHOSES

A girl intending to become a butterfly 101
A girl being transformed into a tree 102
A girl being transformed into a map 103
A girl transforming the world into a fairy tale 104
A girl being transformed into a melody 105
Body transforming into mind 106
A girl turning fear into courage 107
The danger of turning a girl into a poem 109

THE GREAT WORK

Calcination 113
Digestion 114
Fermentation 115
Fixation 116
Filtration 117
Ceration 118
Distillation 119
Congelation 120
Sublimation 121
Union through solution 122
Union through multiplication 123
Union through projection 124

Glosa: The Weather 125

Acknowledgements 127

Notes 129

Baucis and Philemon

Transformation started first with him,
the husband.
Tangles and thickets grew inside his brain,
as a bush, pruned
hard after the glory of flowering,
becomes a mesh
of knobbed and stunted branches. Memories
now a dry nest
where no birds slept. Leaves sealed their stems
at the approach
of winter, their green pigment drained. And she
could only watch

in sorrow, unaware of what was growing
in herself — burl
and wormhole in her lungs, their smooth sponge gnarled
by knot and whorl,
canker and gall. The animal air leaving her at last
on a May day.

We laid the first plume of lilac by her dead hand.
It seemed that she
had become its perfume, filling the city with her breath.
Had become
the scent of linden petals scattering
a drift of bloom
across the humble table in the yard, where
we remembered.

A fragrance he seemed to catch
soon afterward,
not knowing she was gone. This fact too huge
and terrible
to lay in the frail briar of his almost-wordless mind.
But he was able,
still, to ask *Where's Mary?* one day soon afterwards,
lifting his face
like a small dog to a breeze, turning towards
the scent's kiss.

She's coming soon, we told him gently,
not knowing then
the gods spoke truth through us. He smiled
and was content.
Within another week of summer days
his sealed-off leaf
dropped to the ground. Our last gold gift
as we are left.

> 'We ask,' said Philemon to the gods
> 'that I should not live to see her tomb,
> nor she survive to bury me in mine.'
> —*Ovid*

Eve learns endearments

Eve learns endearments

We have not left the garden.
We are locked in
to its stabbing loveliness.

The angels guard the gates.
Their flaming swords are torrents
of solar flare,

writhing a million miles
into black desert
where we could not live.

We are locked in
together in the garden.

The blue sky our fence.
We stare through white palings
of cloud.

~

    I've reached an age
when I call everybody *love*
or *honey* or even, god help me,
sweetie. Indiscriminate endearments
for the young men, young women
who newly populate this earth.

Me, the brisk young bride who swore
she would never use
such silly, sickly names, would choose
a single, cool, distinctive term
to claim affection for her husband.

That task of naming seemed simple then.
A label lettered in thick felt pen
beside each row of cultivated green.

~

Now, I hear my father call the little dog
darlin', lifting each snow-soaked paw
to dry the winter God has introduced
into the garden.

Now time has begun
to waver like snow-snakes
blown across the road, and for him
the territory of names becomes
borderless — *spoon, fork, dog*
separate themselves from stakes.

⌒

Time has stopped. Now
is his only moment.

It becomes the slit in the palings,
through which he watches cold sky

change. Apricot, gold, turquoise.
Those sharp colours of flame.

⌒

I am trapped in this kitchen, kindness
a grater that will not come clean

a cup he will put in the freezer
a spoon he will lose to the breadbox

a kettle he will stupidly make tea in
leaving the teapot to stew coldly

choking on old teabags, a rag
with which he will wipe the floor and then

the bread knife, then insist on washing his chapped hands
yet again for cleanliness.

This is all we can do. Chop plants into small pieces.
Fill soup pots.

⌒

*I feel I should be riding off
somewhere*, he says.

Unhappiness is draped
over his shoulder like the dishtowel.

Where, I ask, internally brutal, wishing
he could/would.

He looks around at the strewn confusion
of carrot peelings, onion shells,

points to the ceiling's pressed cloud.
Answers, *Up there?*

Darlin' It's the Irish sweetening,
his mother's legacy.
She left him
this disease as well.

I ponder mercy.
That time passes.

That we are not bound together
forever, that time will scatter us
into particles, flour through a sieve,
snow on the dark ground.

Time points us out of the garden,
past the swords.

Meanwhile, I am learning
a thing or two from winter
and its incoherence.

Come here, dearie, I say to
the little dog or to my father or
to the neighbour's baby peering
through the fence at
the clear-limbed wonder of 'cat'

We are captives
together in the garden
casting endearments —
our collective net
of love.

Eve's children

Who would have expected
    this first child
would be her father?
    So backwards a birth

◦

What is it like to die, Daddy?
he asked, four years old
and wheezing like an old man —
a delicate child at the time
with lungs like cramped bellows.
The rustle of brown paper,
pasted with mustard and olive oil,
their only poor remedy.

And his father, a small, bow-legged man
rickety from Glasgow, swore
his son would get well, would not follow
those other babies into the dark earth.

Carved a set of small wooden dumbbells,
got him out of bed each morning to stretch his chest
with their slight weight, doused him with water
to make him gulp like a fish from the loch
pulling in the unfamiliar air.

Made him gallop gasping and laughing
over the hills — *Don't let the poliss
catch us.*

Gave him a heart
for the next eighty years.

◦

How he loves to watch the children now,
waves at their pansy faces
like someone who wants to play.

'Can I have a go at that?' he asks
wanting the garden spade, as if it is a toy
he hasn't had a chance at yet.

⌒

Toys. His wooden sailboat —
sixpence spent at Woolworths in a season
of rare affluence, tied at the end of string
to tow behind the steamer, *Jeannie Dean*
as the family all went 'doon the watter.'

In the paddle wheeler's turbulence,
the string snapped. Did he cry?
No. His parents told him
his little boat was off to ports like Africa,
to see the black men loading ships.
'It's going all the places you would like to go.
Wave it goodbye.'

⌒

Together we turn the globe
to look at all the names of places
he sailed to as a blithe young man,
curly-haired mariner.

Addis Ababa, the Gulf of Aden, Alexandria,
(the bars and escapades),
Bombay (the lascars and the stinking fish),
Calcutta, Cairo.

An abecedarium that echoes faintly.
I was there, he says
though he cannot link a name
to pictures, sensations, anecdotes,
maps, emotions, faces.

All snapped and adrift.
Wave them goodbye.

⌒

I spin the globe. Its metal armature
encircles it, a stiff pelvic ring
for the crowning world.

Such a painful labour
to love this intensely old
    round-headed baby

Eve waters the garden

We are making a desert inside the garden.

Perhaps because we yielded
to temptation, ate up gas and oil
as if our acts had no consequence,
and have turned the sky
to a suffocating, carbon-laden trap.

But perhaps this simply is the liturgy
of drought and recovery, warming
and cooling, that our world repeats

and we are not yet wise enough
to understand its purposes.

∽

Years of drought are strangling
the green ash. Its heart hoists water
from root to sky in thin chains —
one molecule clasped to the next,
ten million slender silver columns
stretched to unbearable tension.

The tree's sparse leaves struggle
against the sucking soil, stop
myriad tiny mouths to hold
escaping molecules of moisture.
Every atom irreplaceable.

I assemble serpentine arrangements
of hose. But whatever water
I can give it now
can never be enough.

∽

*There hasn't been any water here
in a long time*, my father says —
a random act of speech dropped
into dinner conversation.

Are you thirsty? I try to guess
source and consequence
without success. He shakes his head.

The irrigation channels of his brain
no longer bathe it in the flow
that carries meaning.

Remember? I ask him,
but the pools shrink incessantly
under this cruel drought. Last year, his stories
were a stagnant repetitious marsh.
Now they are a salt-crazed pan.

∽

But his poems come back
like sudden rain in a desert, one recited line
flowering into the next,
a small recovered miracle.

∽

I have lived in this dry land so long,
still won't accept it.
What god's rain could do so easily,
I labour at.

My father helps lug water in a pot
to transplanted ferns, a petted luxury
as we try to make our tiny garden
inside the desert. *Here*, I tell my father,
pour the water here.

From their pinnate rims,
the lady ferns drop tears.

∽

We could not see without our tears.

They smooth their film across the eyes'
irregularities, a constant mending
of the tiny flaws that pit
the tough, transparent boundary
of cornea.

How I waste this world's energy.
Drive the long ways.
Drive from the garden centre
to the farthest grocery store, drive
to post letters through slots
as far away as possible.

It is the easiest thing to do,
drive so the world goes by his window
like a soothing movie,
a fluid dream.

Eve raises her hand to the tree

We drive the windings
of the ravine road. My wheels touch
the broken line.

You could put him in a home.
The serpent makes a sibilant
kind of sense.
        What kind of test
is this your father sets
with his constant 'I love you,'
his causeless angers.

How much do you owe
for the gift of being formed
at his careless pleasure?

    ∽

In my head, our grocery list —
apples, cherries, oranges. All the tempting flesh
of summer from a distant acre
of the garden.

But the tree of knowledge in my father's head
bears no more
than ragged blue holes of sky.
The poplars strafe by.

    ∽

Not causeless. His angers are fear
blown out like a gas shell round a dying star,
a roiling atmosphere.
He is so afraid we will abandon him.

    ∽

But for now he pushes the shopping cart,
happy in a task he understands,
twists ties around the slippery skins
of plastic produce bags.

Tells me over again,
You're a lovely lassie.

And his love feels like a plastic suffocating bag,
a planetary jail. I need to break its lines
and breathe.

He has set this test for me
and I will fail.

Fall in the garden

It starts perhaps with a sapling
that lights an early flare, burns to gold ash
under the green canopy
still summer-lush.

And then proceeds. Soft maples
become the next candles, light
yellow chambers below the evergreens
in the cemetery.

A measured procession. We absorb
each change in its turn.
Until the oldest elm, at the corner
where a posting-house once stood,
sprays its sky-high fountain of sparks —
a rain of photons on the retina —

and burns out. Now all that lingers
is soft rose in the low bushes,
and cinder drifts.

～

Today, my father begins to pour milk
into a shallow saucer, not his cereal bowl.

Apparently just another twig snapped
in the fire's crackle. But it signals
a soft implosion, opens
a glowing cavern in the architecture
of brain, a vivid vacancy.

A concept of connection has gone,
that 'this' belongs in 'that' — bowl,
mug, urinal. He tries to drink the dice
from the throwing cup
in our game of snakes and ladders.
Object and function linked only
by some toss of association,
and his small peg of identity
slides down the snake's back.

And I, who have been waiting for such progress
almost with impatience, willing
to hurry its winter

turn frantic.

Turn back, turn back,
I silently call out
to his bowed shoulders, as he dabs
patiently at always-present pots.

Don't go further past
the black swords of the pines.
Wear the glory of this world
a little longer, the lit lamp
of the mind.

Eve sings lullabies

Speed bonnie boat

The sailor sprawled on his narrow bunk
in the nursing home

dim window, a porthole
into aqueous light

from the indoor garden of an atrium
where plants from the tropics
make a dusty jungle
that echoes periodically
with bingo calls or the clink
of spoons —
special teas for father's day.

 like a bird on the wing

the caged birds in the atrium
for the diversion of the residents

 'Onward,' the sailors cry
my voice a cracking lullaby

he has been walking, walking
as though leaning into the slant
of a rising deck. Impossible to stop
him pacing this ward the length of a ship
on an unimaginable sea.

Sleep, sleep, sleep, I hum
and like a drumming engine far below,
I hear the prayer, *don't wake.*

Eve studies botany

Sun blooms through the slats
that shield the outdoor patio
beside the nursing home.

My father wears a straw hat
decked with satin ribbon —
a random selection pulled
from the box labelled
'recreation.'

He is drowsing by the flowers —
a spill of white petunias,
nasturtiums the colour of wasps
and trumpets, a scarlet anthem
of salvia, garlands
of holy marigolds.

These brilliant annuals,
so familiar we forget
how marvellous they are,
how far they've travelled
to fill our gardens —
*Africa, Peru, the Caucasus,
the blessed Ganges.*

Beyond the rim of planters,
the parking lot and a high fence
of stiff steel wire. The space beyond it
sliced by utilitarian diagonals.

My father stirs out of sleep.
You're all so beautiful, he murmurs —
raising his hand as if to canonize
the cars, the asphalt, the glowing petals.

And then,
This is paradise.

World spelled backwards

My father was asked
to spell 'world'
backwards — one of the tests.

But he no longer held this globe
of letters in his head.

In the beginning, words.

Then words gone.

And then things
go.

And then the separation of dark and light
will go.

Sun after snow flurries, spring
like someone forgetting
what she's doing, picking up a sock
and staring, purpose interrupted

This is how theology evolves
from primate dominance
to loving father

To the creator who withdraws
from his created world — leaves it rocking
like an ark abandoned on receding waters,
rainbow ephemera
for memories.

Now must I pack up my heart

like a coracle woven of willow,
a nest-boat built
to no central keel.

Each bent branch essential
and expendable.

Memory's daughter

Glosa: Memory's daughter

> *I have to remember everything,*
> *keep track of blades of grass, the threads*
> *of ragged happenings,*
> *and the houses, yard by yard*
> — *Neruda*, 'La Memoria'

The daughters of memory dip their bowls
and dance on the scented mountainside, turn left
then right. Left, the steep descent,
the stone-wound path to Lethe's brown water
where shutters swing on empty houses.
    (Forgetting is the necessary emptying
before a soul can once again begin.) Right,
the trail climbs lightly to the lake whose water
    forgets nothing, ever — Mnemosyne's clear spring.
    I have to remember everything.

The rhythm of my father's mind has changed.
He has gone quiet, sits carefully in company,
alarmed how names now turn and dance away
on feet mysteriously light
and silent. He does not speak about
    this emptiness that spreads
from thought to thought. Instead recounts
his patchwork quilt of poems —
    a verse device to help our musing heads
    keep track of blades of grass, the threads.

Over tea, we sip and dance
around the circle. *I thought I'd hidden it
from you* he says, as if relieved, then promises
that yes, he'll see a doctor. Declares
I'll fight this any way I can. Giant arms spin
    the sunlight at his shoulder. He wrings
our hearts, this White Knight who tilts
his rhyming smile against an enemy so capable
    of severing all the strings
    of ragged happenings.

Later he decides, *I don't want
those doctors poking in my brain.* And we accede.
Oh, you've always been forgetful.
Gentle daughters, pouring him the comfort
of brown water. We leave him waving
      from his crossroad, white hair starred
like a dandelion clock against the grass.
While I turn up the hill. I have the contents
      of every shuttered room to guard,
      and the houses, yard by yard.

Vastly out of scale

Cathedral, Valladolid.
Outside, Yucatan sun a yoke on our weak shoulders,
though the people of Valladolid bear heat lightly
as the yoke of flowers embroidered
on the women's *huipiles*, weightless flutter on white.

We seek relief inside, beneath
the cathedral's towering stone, the ledge high overhead
where a pure white pigeon eyes us down a sunbeam
like a puzzled incarnation.

The Christmas crèche — straw nest, plaster shepherds,
white net stretched up behind and pinned
to a foil star. The baby is painted porcelain,
kicking in the manger, vastly out of scale
with the stiff Virgin in her blue cloak. Mary and Joseph
seem puzzled sparrows by a hatchling cuckoo.
This baby would be the size of a large ham
in Mary's arms.

> And I remember my new brother, holding him
> for a photograph, struggling to prop his floppy baby bulk.
> Squinting, the wind strafing strands of hair
> into my eyes, unable to let pudding-baby go
> so I could scrape the hair aside, cross
> that this was *my* birthday picture
> and the nest felt squashed.

How much easier to love the small,
the dolls scaled to my size. The fairy cups
and saucers diminutive as fingernails.

> Who could love a baby big as a bus?
> Our arms too frail to lift it, its infant wail
> overwhelming.

> Yet this is what is asked of us.

Time scale

Tiny trinity of petals, white announcement —
a minute trumpet, green line tracing its rim.
A call to spring, an invocation
of return.

A bunch of snowdrops in my five-year-old hand
picked from Levengrove Wood. They filled the circle
made by my thumb and fingers,
felt substantial, smelled rapturous.

Now they return, miracles
in my foreign garden. Time has re-scaled
all their dimensions. I find their stems
as fine as wire, their flowers scraps of white,
the faintest trace of fragrance.

But still flowering out of a fist of snow,
to fill this space completely.

Princesses and frog

It lived in a tin bathtub, in a tower
up five stone flights of stairs —
rickety tenement nearly condemned
after a hundred years of fires
in its brick chimneys, old pipes
carrying only cold water
boiled laboriously
in pans on the gas stove.

The princesses watched the frog
lose its tadpole tail and turn
from wiggly almost-insect to
amphibian with gold eyes blinking
on the stone that sat in their bathtub.
(Baths for now taken at Nanna's,
where at least the water ran warm.)
Saw it lose its small brother frog,
unable to live in their tower world.

We have to set it free. So a solemn
Sunday procession went
with the king holding a jar
to the brown water of the trickling burn
that ran along the back
of the housing estate.

And the little frog leaped — one quick turn
into invisibility, instant
and complete. Came not back
with golden ball or kisses
or princely gratitude.
The stream's water cold
as always. So the princesses
climbed back up into their tower
for tea, to be content
with that remarkable act of magic,
bath water turning warm
in the stove's steaming hug.

Deep field experiment

A grain of sand at arm's length. That's how large
    the aperture — pinprick hole in the sky
through which we winnow grain after grain

of light. Focus unwavering. The lens
    reels in the past on a thread
of black sky. We look back at galaxies

minute as rice grains tossed at the wedding
    of infinite and infinitesimal.
A vast field strewn with pale millet seeds.

    Grain, inner pattern. What is there when
stone splits apart. Or wood. When inside
    becomes surface. Look in, look back. My father

in his stiff white overalls, teaching me to grain
a door frame. Comb dragged through paint. Rag wrapped
    around thumbnail, flicks and flecks

to recreate mahogany with umber stain
on sanded pine. Skin on his fingers engrained with paint,
    cracked with chemicals and scrubbing.

Grain. Stained and bundled strands of memory
    combed gently parallel
to lie across your palm like the soft accumulation
    of a daughter's pony tail.
Speck turned silver on night's black emulsion.
    Seed that splits open.

The Gorgon's head

The prognosis is ...
The doctor's voice is down-to-earth
matter-of-fact.
This happens to people.

It's not happening to him.

    Your gut turns to rock.

The internet search turns up
all the grim symptoms

What can you do but turn your head aside,
filter the future through a rearview mirror.

    Don't turn over too many stones.

Swing your sword —
an erratic, untrained heroine —
in the general direction
of hissing.

Penelope weaving

Odysseus has returned. The suitors
are scattered, the children moved away.
The life of the palace has shrunk
to a kitchen, a couch, the figured screen
of the television. Odysseus washes
the teacups.

She will never finish the tapestry now.
They share the bright shapes
woven long ago. Odysseus retraces
the war scenes with his fingers,
the sirens and scattered islands,
tells her again his stories.

Each day, he stands beside her
but can no longer fasten new strands
to the pattern. And sleep unweaves
more and more. Each day starts
over.

Behind the loom, in the unswept corner,
waits the last suitor, patient as a spider.
Not the one most pressing
all those years ago, but now the one
who busies himself weaving
or unweaving. What is he making
on his dark loom, she wonders.
Will that cloth be soft and fine?

Glosa: Parting

> *but there is more*
> *what falls apart is held together*
> *each*
> *atom aligned*
> *— PK Page,*
>   'For Mstislav Rostropovich with Love'

Second childhood.
His brain tearing
its figured lace, forgetting
the tale that held it all together.
She dreads the odour of
    this ward on the second floor.
Sometimes death would be the easier
of partings. Sore, yes,
    but not this sore.
    But there is more.

Always more. She had never cared
for babies. Smelly nappies
drooping from safety pins.
Tedium's ether —
the looking after
    and after, whatever weather
whirled the world skyward.
She dreaded the harness,
    to be told forever
    what falls apart must be held together.

Now his mind falls
apart, eighty
years and words
a repetitious dust.
Over and
    over she tried to teach
now you do
this, this, this. Fastening moments
    each
    to each

And now the parting every time
she leaves the ward —
his small, heartbreaking wave
to the closing door
of the elevator.
    His life confined
and her leaving. Rupture
of what had been
    so long entwined,
    atoms aligned.

Suncatcher

The way an old man sleeps on a winter morning,
light in his hair.
When the sun is bracketed by sun-dogs —
gleams of air,
faint curls of companionship, rainbows
lightly leashed.
When it no longer matters whether
trousers are brushed
clean of cat hair, or match his pilled sweater.
When the cat yawns;
and the small dog noses at her ball, then drowses.
When the day joins
tiles of sunlight with a grout of shadow.
When light's a friend
passing from one window to the next, at this
tessellated end
of another year. The sky one giant crystal
diffracting cold.
The sun out walking its pale dogs on the white paths —
another old
and patient man, passing with a wave beyond
the window sill
where black spruce needles catch splinters of a dream
and hold them still.

What I will need to hold your ashes

A nest of remembered heather
forgotten by its bird.

A doll's house, walls thin as balsa wood,
enameled with leaves and flowers

alive in all the glowing shades of citrus
and ocean.

The brown glass of a whisky bottle,
sullen, square-shouldered sarcophagus.

A dented paint pot, crazed with disuse,
layered in an archaeology of colours.

The velvet casket of a music box — tinkling, twirling stage
for a wobbling ballerina. Tiny screws loose.

A teapot. A tea cup. A drawer of spoons.
A crater on the moon.

And we are here

Here

We did not realize it was so near.
This white, square, unsigned building, mute cube
just across the ragged grass and cinder scree
of a railway line reclaimed for park, where she
and I would take the dog to run.
And we are here.

We did not realize it was so near.
The hearse nosed slowly from its stall
bearing its decorous burden, her fingers laced
white and still above her waist.
We follow. From the car behind, I whisper
I am here.

We did not realize it was so near.
We pass the grocery store where we
would buy our daily breads, then on, as usual,
towards the clinic that should make her well.
But turn a street or two before we get there.
Have brought her here.

How could we know it was so near?
The men are kind, prepare us for the shock
of the industrial, open up the door
to the retorts, warn us of the bump before
the box slides in, a final homage.
And she is here.

We did not realize it was so near,
so thinly separated from the spaces where we live.
But we are here.

Retort as furnace

THE INDUSTRIAL REVOLUTION

Time in a textbook. Revolution
some wheel that went
round and stopped. A sepia period piece —
sweeps in chimneys.
The judder of human machines, bent
at gins and jennies
coking retorts, mine pits, lathes — the dark
Satanic mills,
the grinding courts of chancery.

Labour of laundry tubs, ruckled scrub boards,
lampblack, coal bins,
polished brass. Caps on men and maids.
Bobbed courtesies.
A time romantic because gone from us.
Cut apart,
set in its hand-worked rim/scrim/frame.

But put your hand on her sleeve, here,
and touch it.
Born in nineteen-twenty-three, she
is your spirit
of Eras Past. One handclasp farther takes you
to grandparents
who dandled her. You touch crofters
and clearances,
flax dressers, bleaching fields, famines,
steam engines —
the world that shaped and stamped her.

She lived into this century, to turn the wheel
of millennium
with its lunging gears — not merely as flotsam
washed to the shore
of the present. She is the wave that pulses, casts
itself in a gasp
on the sand. Your wave comes close behind,
you are clasped hands
with foam rings on your linked fingers.

COME TO NATURE

It comes to nature, the ironmasters say
of the metal stirring in the puddling furnace.

Clyde Iron Works — its nineteenth-century chimneys
vast columns of light that blast away the night.
Coarse Scotch pig decomposes in the hot roar
of burning coke, breathes in its fumes —
toxic monoxide sucking out the carbon
that made its cast body brittle. Until
it *comes to nature*.

Experienced artificers of iron
recognize that stiffening consistency of paste
and the puffing of slag on top, as though
some great animal is giving up the ghost,
reducing itself to undiluted elements.

It must become pure enough to be useful.
A residue to be hauled out in huge balls
for shingling. Power hammers beating out
its last impurities and inner fissures
for the sake of spoons and nails and plated ships.

Come to nature. An imperative decreed
by the beings — composite and irreducible —
who purge and engineer, inhale
that dying breath.

VIENNA EXPOSITION, 1873

> *Given a dead body, to resolve it
> into carbonic acid, ammonia and water
> safely, rapidly and not unpleasantly.*
> *— Sir Henry Thompson*

A glass box of ashes and a working model —
a furnace constructed from refracting brick
domed with metal. It is passed by promenades
of frock coats and ladies' lustring frocks.

The Wurstelprater's low-brow carnival
tidied up, crooked streets made straight walks,
fetid homes pulled down. A new channel
excavated for the Danube. And this glass box.

Sanitation the challenge of the century,
an urgency disposing men to work
on disposal of the dead. Cholera laps
the city's feet, beyond the Prater's park.

And further on, Europe's crowded churchyards
suppurate into groundwater. Acids gasp
from the sealed pustules of vaults. More deaths
burgeon ahead, a Malthusian cusp.

Professor Brunetti's exhibit, a retort
to cremate a corpse. Reducing it
to four pounds of pale carbonate
after four hours in a shroud of heat.

A process now made possible by progress —
steel rendered strong enough
to withstand the heat of cannons
for war's shouting mouth.

And the new reverberatory furnace
can render flesh scentlessly to charcoal
out of contact with the flame's harsh tongues.
Transmuted, not unpleasantly. Resolved.

Orphanage as machine

SOLUTION TO A PROBLEM OF PRODUCTION

created when
the ordinary cottage industry
of raising children
becomes inadequate. The raw materials —
the young scraped sore
in the grate of humble funerals,
dazed with crepe.
Mothers' lungs wormholed,
tubercular,
in the crowded, reeking tenements —
the Glasgow slums
or Clydebank shipyards. Air belching smoke
and bacilli.

The product needed: workers. Reliable supply
to man the farms.
Girls for the kitchens and to marry, produce
another hod
of raw material. The system is refined
for turning out
spindles and bobbins, shafts and bits — well-turned
clean-fitting, sound.

The site important. Access to water —
the racing Spey
joined by the tumble of the Lour burn
below Benn Rinnes.
Land enough for buildings, dormitories,
a factory
sprawling tidily. A nearby village — depot
for supplies
and transportation access. A railway platform
with luggage left.

No, never meant to be unkind.
Clean air, Highland
mist, porridge. An orange and a chocolate bar
on Christmas Day.
The stiffening rod of Church. The children
heather-cheeked,
given rough hugs, arithmetic, a chance.
It's simply that
you do not ask the spindle whether this
is what she wants.

MOVING PARTS

The Spey moves swift
in its rocky bed, like the turning links
of a silver chain,
like the linnet's notes
in a rowan bush, or the bubbling throat
of the rain.

They are lined up by the rough stone wall
of a cottage in that Speyside town.
George, the worried eldest. Jim the rebel.
Wee May, and dark-haired Jean.

And how the Spey
has slipped its whirling silver gears
since then.

The small assemblages of family
dismantled. The cries of tiny May
battering at the orphanage's window
as her father walked away.

Machines depend on parts that move
but do not touch. So we repair
the parts that rust and cling together,
stop their wails of fear.

Sisters and brothers prised apart,
assigned by size to varied day-rooms,
to nurseries with narrow cots,
to distant waves in milling playgrounds.

And how the linnet
has turned the water wheel of song
since then.

Reassembled for this photograph,
a chain of beads re-threaded for the day —
a visit from their steel-backed aunt,
brown eggs for tea.

And how the rain
has rusted the machinery of hearts
since then.

FORCE FED

The Canadian waitress slaps a plate
down before her —
a slab of grilled-cheese sandwich, an oozing refectory
of grease, French fries mounded like
a beaver lodge —
enough to see you through the winter
at the far edge
of this new country. How on earth
has she come here
where food is piled up like the Rocky Mountains
to overcome her?

All her life, food was merely nourishment,
a choking duty
after those orphanage years. The plate of tapioca,
its gluey cruelty
returned meal after meal until you ate it,
nauseated.

The dining hall a place of retribution.
Her brother, Jim,
standing on a table there. She could not bear
to look at him,
observe his punishment. He'd tried to run away,
reckless escape
from dominion, was brought back. Eyes down
she faced her plate
of tapioca. Its pale blind eyes glared back
into her tears.

And to this day, a full plate means, not comfort,
but despair –
something from which she cannot run away.
Please, take it back,
she implores a puzzled waitress. *Please,
just take it back,*

FOR THE CHILDREN

The envelopes come flying to her still,
not knowing she is gone.
The apparatus of charity
too slow to catch on
to her flown life. They come
with offerings — memo pads
mechanically embroidered with her name,
address labels, cards and 'tokens
of appreciation.'

She gave to them all. To every envelope
that might help a child — Oxfam,
Unicef, the school-lunch programs,
Save the Children, Hope
Worldwide.

Her small cheques offered
as a tiny counterweight
to the huge machinery of war,
poverty, pain — all that interlocking
mesh of gears.

All the hurting children hers,
and her.

Gas light

THE GAS MANTLE I

Not the flame itself that manufactures light,
but the mantle that surrounds it — the way
a thin crust of air around a planet
rearranges radiation from a nearby star
from black body into bright blue day.

The gas mantle's creation a cascade
of human ingenuity — a cotton web
soaked in a solution of rare earths and left
to harden into a globe. This carbon scaffolding
burned off — no longer needed to support
ceria's incandescent sparkle
in the hot arms of thorium.

So frail is this creation
that clumsy thumbs will easily destroy
its fragile, rigid atmosphere.

THE DANGERS YOU CAN LIVE WITH

The gas jet's hiss of escaping hydrocarbons.
The flame kept licking its lips on the wall
next to her grandmother's glassed-in portrait.
Its eyes that shifted to follow her
(*scared me skinny*)
when she was sent to light the flame's sharp tongue

Seven people in a two-room flat on George Street,
a home made possible
by her widowed father's union
with her steel-spined spinster aunt
twenty years his senior.

Pressure behind the gasometer
relieved by shillings.

Creaks and joyless groans forced
from the hole-in-the-wall bed,
across the kitchen where she and her sister slept
by the dull smoulder of coal fire.

Her own body a skinny tube. Too thin,
she thought in an age where glossy pictures
displayed pleasing roundness. Sharp apples
new under her nightgown.

Fondled by an uncle when she was sent
to deliver dumplings — but she slipped
away from his confining weight and out the door,
hissing as she went.

MY MOTHER AS HISTORY

Browsing the boardwalked nostalgia
of the historical site, caught between sepia
and amber — yellowing paper on walls,
smell of yellow soap in narrow halls,
tins of golden syrup, toffee-coloured bottles
for patent medicines, butter paddles,
mangles, oilcloth, cauldrons; and the patch
of cardboard by the round-buttoned switch
that describes this as the first home in the city
to be lit by electricity.

A spark of indignation passes
from my mother to the wall, bifocal glasses
fixed on the sign's bland patronage.
That's not history, she says, on edge
with insult. *I remember when they brought
power to the orphanage.* The bright watts
of memory flare — the switch pulled
for the ceremony, Canon Woolfe
doing the honours, the glow of gas mantles
blown out. The fat, bright cheeks of glass bulbs.

She doesn't want this memory reclassified
as 'history.' A quaint lamp set aside.

THE GAS MANTLE II

The carbon scaffolding is burned away,
a vapour in the blue atmosphere.
The shape of my mother in this world
is now an kind of incandescence in the mind —
a flowering of light, a globe
I form around the flame
she made alive.

The Movies

PERSISTENCE OF VISION

Action sliced so thin it freezes
into a single frame, a picture
in a Zoetrope. Revolving drum,
a slit, a source of light
and the stopped motion re-starts.
The eye reassembles tiny increments
into continuous flow.

A parlour curiosity, Victorian novelty,
those flickering dreams. And yet
its turning drum created
a kind of heat. Hold a strip
of newly invented celluloid nearby
and it bursts into light —
around the world, horses dash
across screens as wide as walls.
The feverish crank of cameras,
reels flying through the projector's
thin, bright, 'now.' Cowboys,
Cupid's bows and swashbucklers
are animated, twenty-eight frames
per second, the heated friction
of narrative, its persistent visions.

OH, ROSE MARIE, I LOVE YOU

She loved the love stories.
The talkies then so new, younger
than her own young life.

Sound now printed as a barred scrim
beside the sprocket holes
along a strip of images,
meshing cleverly with movement
as Nelson Eddy belted out the long, strong notes
of *Rose Marie* like a conveyor belt.
Sound drenching landscape
as if it were quite reasonable to fill
Canadian forests with a full-blown orchestra.

Her birthday treat — taken to the pictures
in the afternoon. Rialto Cinema
on College Street, the new film
Maytime. Her grandfather paid down
sixpences for tickets
and they entered the flicker of story
half-way through. Jeannette MacDonald
as the ball's belle, Nelson Eddy waltzing her
around spring-time's ribboned pole.
May enchanted.

They watched until the end, and then
until the point where they came in.
That's it, May, said her granddad.
We've seen it all. But she pleaded
to see that scene again, and then another
until her patient grandfather
got cross and said, *I'm going now.*
you'd better come along.
But she refused, sat there alone
in the palace of repeatable dreams.
Watched to the end
then round again.

For once, the princess had refused
to leave at midnight.
She waltzed home at last, in thrall
to the Presbyterian stepmother's scolds
but did not care. Her feet were on petals.
She had been to the ball.

MAYTIME

We bring back *Maytime*, my mother and I,
iridescent
on a DVD's whirling circle.
In the present,
the past lifts from its static, stuttered pattern
of pits in plastic,
the way time's phase transition melts the solid,
inelastic,
into flow with the ruby laser-tip of 'now.'

We watch, content,
the end. The old lady slipping into sleep below
the tanglement
of blossom-laden branches. The young lover's ghost
bending down,
reaching out transparent hands to her.
Music blown
around them like returning swallows — *Sweetheart,
sweetheart, sweetheart,
will you love me always?* And her young self rises
to step apart
from that old, discarded body. She takes his hand,
unhesitating
ghost. A different phase transition — the solid
sublimating
straight to air, something that inhabits neither
solid nor stream,
but time itself — its pattern of pits and lands.

We turn the machine
off. The notes and images have re-condensed
on the silver skin
of the DVD, like a film of quick mercury
coating glass.
I click the disk safely inside the hard fact
of its cover, pass
it to my mother. She takes it, tucks it
in, at random
on the rack below my father's picture.

His sad phantom
still walks a dementia ward nearby,
the lost glow
of shared lives fading from his pitted mind.

Still, we know
that we can watch this tale at least, whenever
we want its hands
held out to us, its springs, its silvered pasts,
its happy ends,

its promised ghosts.

SONG

She sang like the linnet in rowan bush,
like the mavis
    opening its book of song.
In her nest at the top of the tenement's tree
she sang to her downy young.

She sang at home, a slender bird
in her native wood
    at the pasture's edge.
Applause round a table at supper time
was her largest stage.

Songs about ash groves, western isles,
heiland hames —
    the well-worn tropes.
Our enduring delight in birdsong springs
from its birl of familiar notes.

Never caught on loop or reel,
that sweet, high voice
    on the family's bough.
Oh, if the years could spin around
    and I could hear it
        now.

Transport

ROMANCE

The *Cutty Sark*, great clipper ship
luffing in the Tasman Sea,
her sails' plump cheeks
gone sagged and wrinkled.
She is a world away
from her place of birth, the cradle berth
of the shipyard where the Leven
meets the Clyde

when the Royal Mail Steamer, *Britannia*,
heaves into view. Fastest
in the Peninsular and Oriental Line,
her smug screw
spins, winds held tight
in her engine room's Aeolus cave
The steamer passes *Cutty Sark*, her crew
waves goodbye to the waning moon
of the clipper's curved hull.

But *Cutty Sark*'s captain waits, wisely,
catching the scent of wind
in his left eye. And with the night
the god of winds turns tail,
flicks the frayed rope fastened to the bowsprit
and away she goes again.
Every shred of *Cutty*'s shift spread,
all of Aeolus' children in her sails
from t'gallant to spinnaker,
their cheeks firm and young again.

Britannia's second officer looks out
onto the moonlit ocean, aghast,
and writes in the ship's log:
*Overhauled and passed
by a sailing ship.*

Yes, it is romance — the run to Sydney Harbour,
the steamer pulling in to Circular Quay
and the tall ship there already, masts
swaying to the waves' applause,
the steamer's passengers cheering
their own ship's loss.

Romance is real,
even if the shipyard on the Clyde back home
now rings with the *ack∙ack∙ack* of rivet guns
not the thick thwack of carpentry,
and the slabbing mills of Glasgow
are rolling plate on plate of steel
to be cut in the shape of ships.

Even though the steamers' penned winds
and stubby masts
will overhaul all sail, now and then
Tam O'Shanter's mare can leap across
the Brig O'Doon a nose ahead of witches,
and sometimes we are overtaken
by the past.

CAMOUFLAGE

She seems to go unseen,
shy and fiery,
a young woman watching from a bridge.

The estuary
of the Clyde shrouded, its gloaming water
under cloud,
while the people of the shipyards gaze
silent and proud
as the great grey Queen slides past them, ghost ship
in camouflage.
The Queen Elizabeth, Clyde-built.
Her maiden voyage
secret, racing to America, towards
the New York piers
where packed soldiers, jostling, kit-bagged,
await their wars.

She seems to go unseen, camouflage
her world. The nights
blacked out. Imitation cardboard barracks
on the sere heights
of the Old Kilpatrick hills, distraction for
the German bombs.

At twenty, she is silent, in disguise
and no one comes
like her sister's handsome soldier beau,
to find and woo.

BOOK PASSAGE

List of passengers. The booklet's print unfurls
a scroll embossed
in gold, and the lion rampant on a shield —
Cunard Line crest
in red and black, to match the liner's
blazing funnel.

She has booked passage on this ship —
high arched tunnel
to her future. The booklet's first page printed
with this day's date,
April sixteenth, nineteen fifty-seven,
and then a freight
of names in tourist class. Each letter
of the alphabet
commences a chapter of emigration, hope
its sharp bowsprit.

First passage of the season. At last
the ice has cleared
from the St. Lawrence and the port of Montreal,
her trip deferred
till spring's release. Now, this encyclopedia of ship
holds three short lines
for Mary and her two small daughters
who bob behind
like the tugboats pictured at the liner's skirts.
Story-books glow
in their arms — Noddy books and fairy stories bought
from shops in Glasgow
especially for the journey, not to be read till now.

Books shining new
like the R.M.S. *Saxonia*, Clyde-built,
her curved bow
plated in John Brown's yard. Already she's a chapter
about to close,
written over by the year-round drone of aircraft.
Stiff wings will ease
her foaming turbines aside. But for now, she holds
eight hundred names.

'*Miss Carol.*' '*Master James.*' '*Craftsman Owen.*'
The steel chains
of naming to be reworked in different orders
across an ocean
of possibility. Mary passes through
the ruled commotion
of boarding with that other book of passage
tight in her hand —
her dark-blue passport, its cardboard binding
with the gold stamp
of the Britain she is leaving behind. She climbs
steep-slanted stairs
from the tender to the liner's deck, so high above.
For now, her cares
are packed with their belongings in a tea-chest,
in the hold below

while the book of passage takes her to reunion —
the clasped folio
of her husband's arms, waiting at the end
of this short tale
to be written in the curl of wave and wind.

Clocks

THE UNIFORMITY SYSTEM

Yankee clockmaker, Eli Terry, wracked
with an order for four thousand clocks.

Realizing identical parts
would build identical movements.

Three years setting up a factory.
Steam and wheels, lathes and jigs

to cut interchangeable pinions.
Pawls and ratchets. Collets. Crutch pins.

Then the burst — four thousand clocks
assembled in that last year of his contract.

Ticking uniformly in wooden boxes
on mantels all across America.

And thousands more to come. A flood
suddenly affordable. A good.

ESCAPEMENT

The clock on her mantel was a wedding present,
Its polished wooden case a standing wave
wrapped over the dial. The round glass cover
a cupboard door that swung open,
clicked closed after winding.

Ticking innards behind. Escapement
converting the smooth force of spring
into quantized stops and starts.

The tiny flat at the top of Heggie's Building,
her first own home. The fresh-painted walls,
the modern fireplace — installed
by the young couple. Ridiculous to spend
twenty pounds on this decaying tenement.

But she went down on her knees
for gratitude, for this little cupboard
where she could set out love.
The children reading comics on the rug
before the grate. Her husband coming
up the stairs from work.

Freedom can be as small as this. A door to close.
Escapement turning with a tick.

ASSEMBLY LINE

Children restless in a wriggled line
beside the boot-to-bonnet hubbub of buses.
A hopscotch of thick kilts.
Each child issued with a clock-shaped badge
cut from coloured construction paper
and pinned to woolly Fair-Isle jumpers.

The children of a thousand employees
in the Westclox factory
offered this junket up to Kelvin Hall
to see the circus.
Her two girls among them, the eldest
disappointed in the dull brown
of the badge assigned to her.

Mary waved goodbye, turned to her shift —
the work of taking things apart, clock movements
ill-made on the plant's brand-new assembly line
that constructed ten thousand clocks a week.
Her quick fingers unscrewed face plates
stamped 'Made in Scotland,' tossed
steel wheels into boxes for re-use.
Minute hands by the hour.

The post-war blast of production
made cheap time a priority — alarms and chimes
needed for conveying workers to their shifts.
The old clocks all run down by war.

Mary's pay cheque put aside each week
to help afford their passage overseas,
to slip this particular chain
of being, this conveyor going
to a dull brown destination.

While the children — that bright bulge
of post-war assembly —
watched the sparkling ballerinas
go round and round the ring
balanced on their silver-backed horses,
while the clowns flipped themselves
through linked hoops, and the elephants
shuffled their trunk-to-tail train.

Then looked round for their clock-colour buddies,
were instructed to take hands, form chains
climb back aboard their line
of puffing buses.

Explosives

HELL'S KITCHENS

Wind stood still in the foggy hollows
of a battlefield — call it Quatre Bras, Waterloo,
Pea Ridge or Lundy's Lane —
where black-powder soot made soup
of unstirred air.

A few volleys
of clear fire before soldiers were lost,
chucking mud to glut the barking cannonade
in Hell's third circle. Soldiers choked
in the purgatorial broth, waiting for a spoon of breeze
to shift the clouds
for a glimpse of what was aimed at them —
figures fleeting in the gaps
above the fouled barrels of their guns.

Chemist Schönbein, Basle,
eighteen-forty-six, in his Swiss kitchen
(where his wife didn't want him mixing
his malodorous acids)
grabs her cotton apron to mop
spilled spirit of nitre.
Hangs it tidy on the oven door to dry.

Continues with his measuring weights
and beakers, whirls at the flash
when the apron detonates.
Not a trace of solid left behind.

He has discovered gun-cotton,
a few atoms swapped out
of the placid recipe for cellulose.
Now aprons, dishtowels, the inert
rags of resentment underneath the sink
can become brilliantly unstable,
instant gas.

Devil's Porridge. A vat, violent and volatile
of nitroglycerin and nitrocellulose,
mixed slowly to a lethal jelly.
Stirred more carefully than witches round
a loathsome brew. *Fire burn
and cauldron bubble.*

Thickened to a paste, two unstable substances
slowly kneaded into temporary quietude,
then extruded through nozzles —
a dreadful icing to decorate the war.
Snipped to the right lengths to fit shells,
cartridges, guns' blunt muzzles.

The chemists' kitchen witcheries translated
to vast cauldrons in munitions factories.
Thousands of workers apprenticed
to this cookery. Giant stoves
in Nitrate Hills, columns and separators,
the drowning tanks, the washing houses.

Women circling the piles of finished cordite
picking handfuls from each batch in turn,
to pack well-mixed boxes.
Double, double, toil, trouble.

But for the deadliest phase, only women
'of mature age'. Not a giddy girl,
not a boisterous man. Not a hairpin.
Not a ring, a fastener, a good-luck charm
to strike a spark in this fume-drugged room
with its hellish gruel.

Just *the auld maids in P6*,
who stir and press and watch
the toads' eyes shine.

THE BALLAD OF RED CLYDESIDE

Yellow the skin of the lyddite workers
— yellow as lye, yellow as mustard —
from the acid they packed in artillery shells,
staining their hair, staining their nails.

The nitric dioxide boiled off in clouds
— brown as the mud in the trenches of France —
toxic spume under cover of night
from the bunkered works on the Leven's banks.

'Canaries' they called them — imported girls
turned yellow by bitter picric salts.
Brought here to live in the tattered strip
of 'The Huts' — like cages for sallow birds.

Just one in the chain of munitions works
grinding through Glasgow — the cannon's bore,
the armourer's plate, the chemical fire.
Laborious mine shaft essential to war.

Red the blood
of their soldier sons
and their husbands felled
by the blazing guns
while their women worked.

Black were the landlords' bowler hats.
Black their boots. Black their hearts
as the soot-sickened chimneys they rented out.

The rents going up as the workers arrived
to blacken their hands on the war's behalf.
Twenty percent in a single year's gouge.

The soldiers' wives unable to pay
from their slender purses, while husbands lay
legless or armless or shell-shocked abroad.

Black was the ink on the landlords' rolls.
Black was the ink of the newspaper howls
in the socialist press. 'Maraud! Maraud!'

> *All Glasgow red*
> *as the open roar*
> *of a furnace door*
> *and the flame seen clear*
> *to London.*

White were the packets of pease and flour
and laundry soap pelting the bowlers
when Mrs. Barbour's Army turned out
with rolling pins and pokers
against the Sheriff's officers
with their vile eviction notices.

> *Red the flag*
> *in George's Square.*
> *Red as Russia.*
> *London scared*
> *and needing guns.*

So the law came up, the law came down.
The landlords found their fingers bound
to keep them out of the workers' purses.
Sometimes the tide of power reverses.

War went on.

THE TORY CANDIDATE COMES TO CALL

in her well-cut tweeds, a knock at the door
of the flat where the bairns are colouring
on the carpet in front of the fire,
and the pots are preparing to boil.

Mary answers the knock,
and she's a fragment of cordite
under the rap of a hammer,
when the candidate, polite

and bloody condescending,
asks for her vote, *Mrs. Major, to get
those Labour MPs out of parliament.
They'll ruin the country.*

The Red Clyde boils in Mary's veins.
*You with your handbag and pearls.
You'd ruin the workers.*
Her girls, her seed pearls, look up.

She's not about to give back
the small new monthly cheque,
family allowance, that lets her buy
her daughters their good oxfords.

The would-be member of parliament
is sent with a flea in her ear
back down the tenement's stone stairs
like a ladder down silk stockings.

RED MARY

Here she is at eighty.
The son-in-law with whom she lives,
teasing, calls her Red Mary.

Her daughter lectures tiresomely on
the political nuances of socialism
vs. social democracy.

Her son in Ontario bosses workers,
taking home pay
she could never dream of.

All their words that try to cloud
her persistent vision — that the world must be
something brighter, justice and a sky
blue as her eyes for everyone.

They can't wear down that ruby point
with which she plays her life over,
that temper spurting pyrotechnical,
her inner crystal
that keeps the watch ticking.

Camera

LATENT IMAGE

> 'My dearest Miss Mitford, do you know anything
> about that wonderful invention of the day, called the
> Daguerreotype? ... It is the very sanctification
> of portraits, I think.'
> — Elizabeth Barrett Browning to
> Mary Russell Mitford, *1843*

Light held still
by salts and silver. A thin metal salver.
Layered crystals
of halide, where the glimpsed image waits,
the faintest ghost
of potential haunting the camera's dark room.
Metempsychosed
by the photographer's dim baths, where atoms
of pure metal
creep from their compound lattice,
gather, settle
into the pattern sketched by that first flash
of aperture.

The way a mind gropes towards memory —
patient capture
of detail, through laying down
minute changes
in molecule, synapse. The process strengthens signals,
rearranges
the fragile glass plate of record.

Caught light clusters
around a figure in lace, the curve of a dead child's face,

stilled gestures.
Life departed. The Victorians so willing
to look again
and again at death. This portrait, perhaps
the only one
ever taken. We look aside, look slant, with creeping
modern distaste
at light's irreversible reversal into dark,
the latent face.

THE STUDIO PHOTOGRAPHS

Stationary mounds of cumulus behind their heads —
tendrils and wisps on a painted sky
that stays the same in every picture.

They lean against the same scrolled banister
wound with vines. Two pretty girls caught
in wartime's aura of black and white.

The clouds are fixed
as the shutter drops between this moment
and the next.

It is the sisters' faces that transform
softly, one into the other,
below the nimbus of waved hair.

Jean's eyes wider, darker.
Mary's face turned slightly more aside,
her cheekbones finer.

No lens reveals what happens after.
How one face will outlive the other
by forty years, creased

into the cirrus-drift of age —
those faint streaks that trail after grief,
remembering its passage.

THE ACCIDENTAL SNAPSHOT

It held its place in the photo album,
year after year, a family joke.
The one perfectly composed
but accidental photo — a loaf
of Weston's bread, bright
in its red-and-blue wrapper (the still-new
colours of photography) snapped
on a picnic at Riverdale Zoo.

The little brother scolded
for playing with the shutter, pressing
its fidgety button where the camera sat,
its blind eye closed on the picnic table.
Images so precious to develop,
too expensive to waste.

This close-up perfectly in focus
while the pictures of Mary and her children
are distant, blurred with the slight motion
as the camera's eye shuts.

One preserved detail
random, apparently irrelevant.
Memory's opened eye, its strange
selection from the flux.

DIAGNOSTIC IMAGING

CHEST X-RAY

The rib cage arched like a church window
to frame her heart, now grown too large.

Her ribs are slender, spectral mullions. Her bones
faded from the centre, only their outlines clear.

The lovely volute of clavicle, its curved scroll.
The arm bone with its rounded finial.

But the lungs are clouded, not the clear sky
we should see through this frame. Mist rises.

CT SCAN OF LUNGS

Slices carved by radiation, a progression
down through chest, thorax. Bloodless dissection.

Blood vessels gleam, dots in cross-section.
Points of dye-induced light.

The lungs appear first as small dark regions,
nebulae against a milky way.

But in later cuts, the blessed, air-filled dark gives way
to a tendrilled mass. *Tumour or fluid*

says the doctor. Though fluid would lie smoother,
a grey meniscus on the lung's curved border.

Probably both. The cancer's fuzzed stars
and its liquid secretions, its vile milk.

CT SCAN OF BRAIN

A Rorschach ink-blot, symmetrical,
defined by edges, not interior.

Its pale mottlings are featureless
even to this invading eye.

Crimped notches pink its perimeter,
the ventricles are dark reversals at its centre.

These are the shrinkages of age
says the doctor. *Definitely an older brain.*

Where is the tiny lady in a lilac hospital gown?
The dear shell of the face? This portrait's frame?

FULL-BODY SCAN

She lies like a saint on a tomb, arms at her side.
Points of light star her frame.

One on the left wrist, like the radium dial
of a watch. Others like nails in knees and shoulders.

Old injuries says the doctor. Not likely
to be new sites of metastasis.

Her one remaining kidney
is another point of light, processing dye.

The pelvis fluoresces. The harp-line of it
so beautiful, the resounding bone.

These, the last pictures of her life.
She is receding still deeper into time,

into the past
and far into the future.

Lullaby for my mother

>*Hush-a-by my broken bough.*
>*Hushaby, my cradle. Sleep, bunting, sleep.*

I hold her at the end of this duet
we have been singing all our lives.
How I wish I could remember
her young face floating over mine, her eyes

wide with the rhythm of our mutual lilt,
antiphon of smile and coo.
'Bye-bye bunting.' 'Peek.' Gentle piggies
all the way home. *'And who's a good girl now?'*

>*Hushaby my broken bough.*
>*Hush-a-by, my cradle.*

I hold her at the end of this duet.
Her fingers wander in the air,
the way a newborn will consider
movement in an unfamiliar atmosphere.

Tiny bird. At times she grows distressed.
Hush, I croon, anguished at the sleep
that will release her from this nest,
this tattered cradle. My good girl, all the way
>home.
>*Sleep, bunting, sleep.*

Time is how

Time is how

Time is how one thing becomes another.
Fish evolves to take the form of seaweed
and hide in fronds of kelp. Feather
emerges from scale, begins to breed
the radiant array of plumages.
One cell that senses light grows into eye.
All the carefully elaborated lineages
by which bacterium becomes a fly.

Time, infinitely patient, joins
then separates. Enjambment, lines
that break apart. The fish is not a plant.
I am not bird, nor ever could be —
have not the power to recant
the million generations that encage me.

Lines that break apart

Arcadia is burning. As if its king,
Lycaon — turned to wolf by Jove,
as Ovid's story goes — is returning
to raven on its woods and olive groves.
Smoke propels across the Peloponnese
visible even from the satellites,
those gods'-eye lenses hung in space.

Fire replicates, gorges appetites,
sustains its roaring body and seeds
its wild posterity on driven wind.

But fire is a vacant metaphor for life. It needs
no ancestry, no past. It must depend
on fuel and spark, external accident.
Not on the wolf's incendiary intent.

The fish is not a plant

How Ovid would have loved *Pycodurus*
equus — the Leafy Sea Dragon. The tale he'd tell!
Slender fish nymphs begging *Oh, secure us,*
Father Sea, cowering in a field of kelp
and pleading to the god of roiling
change. He turns the scales of their soft armour
to long fronds for camouflage, foiling
the snapping, seeking animals whose hunger
goes without end. But then comes the high cost
of rescue. Motion becomes drift, not dart,
slow turn and tumble. The nymphs are lost
when other predators invade their seaweed ark
to snatch them for aquariums. Their fins
now shrunken, the bound feet of concubines.

One thing becomes another
(by turning first into itself)

Line's
puzzle.
Syllable
combines,
brings
adenine
to thymine.
Strings
a grammar,
a street,
a beat,
stammers,
repeat.
Repeat.

Enjambment

click	lock
bond	bound
molecule	clock
chimed	chained
spiral	mirror
twinned	twined
copy	error
model	mould
join	sever
told	re-told
codon	codex
cleave	fold
fate	luck
lock	click

The million generations

Mitochondrion — minute time capsule,
tiny furnace for burning oxygen
slowly, molecule by molecule.
Remnant of that first bacterium
to crack this art of cracking energy
from elemental bonds. Now it has become
our captive, a coated organelle
tucked inside the busy confines of a cell.

This separate ring of DNA passed down
the generations, only through the female line.
Inheritance of hearth, carried
like a live coal in a box of moss-lined horn.
This bound circle we inherit
from our mothers — the ability to burn.

The radiant array of plumages

*And who could believe such wonders emerge
out of eggshells*. From hummingbird to ostrich —
that mammoth chicken, a fluffy juvenile
that just gets bigger, won't grow up. In denial.
Golden pheasant, blonde crest pouffed back
and jacket glitzing like a Vegas lounge act.
Can-can curvaceous bottoms flocking
on flamingos. Juno's peacocks cocking
stars on the marquee of their tails.
Fairy wren, blue pirouette. Nightingales,
brown flight wrapped around a throat.
And here by my window, the black-capped
chickadee wearing his tiny yarmulke. Magic
winter's wisecrack, my branch-borne comic.

Time, infinitely patient, joins

The capacity for attachment
evolves, begins with solitary microbes.
A chance stickiness of molecules
latches on to food. DNA encodes
these tiny grappling irons,
hands them on. Microbes form rafts,
colonies of self-interest. One cell
divides, sticks to itself, learns the craft
of joinery. This gift of affinity —
to become part of a larger whole.
The cell becomes studded with buttons,
hooks and eyes, keys and keyholes.
So great a revolution this is,
turning greed into kisses.

Have not the power to recant

Birds return to flightlessness on islands.
Rimmed by the perimeter of ocean,
pigeon becomes dodo. The wide bands
of sea seem inexhaustible protection.
In such a demi-paradise,
the urgent investment in escape
turns to scrabble on the ground, the ties
of nests, eggs. The future is opaque
to genes picked over for advantages
in such little Edens, where
danger only flickers at the edges
of an island planet within its moat of air.
A thinly margined realm, behind its berm.
A space of no return.

Begins to breed

Oxygen does time
for its violently reactive behaviour.
Locked up in rust and oxide, assigned
to cells within the planet's fortress mantel.
While Nature continues the endeavour
of building her domain, mechanical
and plan-less. Until small liberators slip keys
into the compound — the blue-green bloom
of algae, conspiring. Oxygen steals free,
is slapped back in irons, red beds
of weathered rock. But the algae resumes
its subversions, sucks in CO_2, unthreads
its tiny screws and looses oxygen to breed
mindlessly the air where minds can breathe.

One cell that senses light grows into eye

Step by step the whole contraption
of pinhole, lens, reflector, brain
to reassemble signal into pattern
of line and colour, edge and plane.

Initial sensor so exquisite
it registers each singlet hit
from light's lightest unit.
But that's the easy bit.
More essential is the tangled circuit
that lurks behind, needed to interpret

and construct the scrying eye of forecast.
to let us catch the indistinct glint
of sails on the horizon, past
the breaking dazzle of the moment.

I am not bird nor ever could be

Bohemian waxwings, small cinnamon nomads,
flock to the clean snow of my roof. They toss
its crisp powder down their throats, across
their quick, exquisite wings. Red drops
glow on feathers like candy hearts. Luminary
in the lacework Valentine of February,
they cluster on branches like the berries
they love to feast on — the dried-crimson clots
of rowan. Then lift as one, caught
in some wind I cannot feel, a spirit messaging
among them to form a cloud — a swirling cell
encircling the intent of individuals
with twittering communication. In winter's frost,
I ponder such shared sweetness. And its loss.

Feather emerges from scale

We are built from the outside in.
First came surface.
The proto-animal's protective membrane
— its shell of cells —
puckers into fissure, cavern, orifice.
Appetite compels
soft layers there to harden into conodont.
Tooth swells
into bone. Outside, skin's protean gradient
continues its twists
and tucks. Underlayer pinches into gland
and shaft, bursts
into duct, hair, feather. Surface layers quilt
nipples, pores — shared plan for quill and milk.

The generations that encage

Violently reactive
in our ability to burn,
we form a protean gradient
in the planet's skin
Not through incendiary intent,
but as if mindlessness arises
out of mind. We have become
gods of roiling change, trapped catalyzers.

The future is opaque
for fragile demi-paradises.

What can open the past's cage? Fate?
Luck? Or must we repeat, repeat, the damages
caused by our gift for affinity? We beg escape
from our carefully elaborated lineages.

Metamorphoses

A girl intending to become a butterfly

Monica, in the Thai restaurant, stars
in her eyes, enraptured
by the dancer in a dress unfolding like a chrysalis.

'Isn't she beautiful, Aunty Alice?'
    she breathes, trying to copy a butterfly
gesture of the fingers.

Ten years old.
Disease is pulling at her spine the way an archer
draws a strung bow. Her shoulder blades
are the beginning of wings.

Earlier that day, the butterfly house —
Monica holding out her hand, eager and steady,
for all the nameless wings to light on.

One that drooped like ivory lace, a Victorian fichu.
Another that flew
in a black-and-scarlet tarantella around her head.
One absolutely sheer
with one blue spot, like naughty lingerie.

Monica is longing to emerge
in all these costumes,
wardrobe mistress of wings.

A girl being transformed into a tree

Hospital ward. Our votive offerings
clutter utilitarian furniture:
holy water in a plastic bottle,
a tiny icon of the Dalai Lama, packets
of organic tea and vials of aromatic oil,
the glass fonts filled with lilies
and small, infolded roses. We are praying
to all the faces of the faceless god.

Monica asleep. IV tubes trickle
their clear sap.

I touch her face, remembering
the eager two-year-old at the crest
of the playground slide, her delight
in climbing to the highest step,
her headfirst shrieks of glee.

Now, the too-beloved of the selfish god
with his cruel golden bow,
she is the nymph in headlong flight —
a race two decades in the running.
Her heel still just eludes the grasp
of the ravisher.

She is growing rooted to the spot. Her limbs
so inhumanly slender, her body a slim-branched trunk.
Tender bark binds her chest,
muffles her voice.

A mask sends its constant thrust
of air into her lungs. Asleep, her cheeks and throat
puff slightly under its pulse. I think of a newborn mouse
or bird. And her hair still spills exuberance.

I clutch these signs of animal life, amulets
to ward off the laurel-bound god.

A girl being transformed into a map

Monica's bones. Rubbing oil and lavender
on her back, the lumbar curve so deep
it's like a pocket. As though the map of bones
is stretched and pulled
like a delicate topological experiment:
> *'This must*
> *remain connected*
> *to this,*
> *but how far can*
> *you twist it'*

Lavender drowses on my fingers.
Outside the hospital, the heavy scent of summer
is foreign, upside down. I left snow in soft mounds
on a dark morning to fly here. Video screens
in the plane's stagnant air
were our evidence of motion —
the maps that tracked our path past Fiji
towards Australia's hunched shoulder.
The scent of coffee stretched into the cabin
like a yawn. The sleepers began to unfold themselves
and I thought how continents drift, slowly re-articulate.
We deduce their evidence of motion
from rock striations, fossil bones.

Monica's neck is sore. I drop
more almond oil on my palm, reach into the deep fissure
between spine and scapula.

We are maps pulled apart,
drawn together.

A girl transforming the world into a fairy tale

Once upon a time, not so long ago …

Monica in her wheelchair. We are believing in magic.
She turns the staring children into frogs, the sidelong glancers
into lizards. We are alone in the village, except
for the flower seller who gave her red roses,
and the café waiter who is fair and charming.

We have just bought fairy wings — a present
for her little sister; though Monica now knows
that star-tipped wands do not work spells.

Instead we order reckless cocktails,
strawberry daiquiris, pink and frilled as tutus,
and giggle over how we'll look going home
driving a wheelchair over the limit,
shedding fairy dust from her packages.

Her scornful 'They won't run me over,'
when entreated to move up on the sidewalk,
watch out for the rough spots.

She is making time stop like traffic.
Her poems are full of stars and holes.

A girl being transformed into a melody

All night at the hospital, the peeping
of monotonous equipment with its dull red eyes.

Now on the back step, brushed
by overhanging leaves,
I am teased by the riddle of wind chimes.

Languid combinations repeat, almost
repeat. A single note struck thrice
like some avant-garde composition. I realize
this melody sounds intentional because
the notes are artificially constrained —
only a few sounds possible, chosen to harmonize
one with another.

The breeze turns stronger in the mid-day heat
like a sleeper restless under blankets.

Frustrating ... the wind-chime tunes never resolve,
never finish. Melody starts up, but
just when you want it to repeat — just when
a composer would insist that it repeat — it
stops. Not human music after all.

Or all too human. Our lives so full of repetition,
so completely unrepeatable.

Body transforming into mind

We are awkward puppeteers,
trying to put our muscles to her mind.

Move my elbow in closer, she directs.
Pull the pillow back.

She's tired of being told of Stephen Hawking,
how free the mind can be.

I don't want to be a super-cripple
she says crossly. Doesn't want to dance
on any other strings.

She wants a body like any other girl's.
Wants a lover. Wants to pull her own strings.
Wants the boys dancing.

A girl turning fear into courage

She leans her forehead
on her beautiful, thin hand —
our lady of the camellias —
while the technician tangles her hair with white gum
to fasten electrodes.

Thin coloured wires are tied up
in a zany pony tail — all the kids will want one.
We trundle down the hall, trailing
intravenous poles and electric cords
to where her sleep will be monitored
by another bank of oscillating dials.

But Monica is silent, doesn't want to close
her eyes just yet. At last she asks,
    Will I wake up again?
And I realize how black a shape she stares at.

On ancient vases, Hades faced away —
the living should not intercept death's gaze.
But tonight her eyes are locked in his.

We offer comforting distractions.
Explain we're simply trying to find out
how to help her lungs get through the nights
so she will go on
awakening each day. Until
she murmurs,
    I know I'm being silly.

Then tells me of her dreams — the one about
arriving at a party, all her friends
crowding round to celebrate, calling out
'We're so glad you're here.'

I stroke her hair, to keep my fingers busy.
You look like a telephone switchboard,
I say to make her laugh.

I feel like one, she answers, returning
the favour

The danger of turning a girl into a poem

Too many farewells. The hospital room,
the airport. My sister.

Now below me, the coast
with its handkerchief of surf waving goodbye,
the clouds turning their backs on us
to go about their business.

Monica back there —
Thou still unravished bride —
the tale unfinished, the frieze
on the Grecian urn, figures caught on the cusp
of hope and fear, the round shoulder of the vase
that turns away.

But I cannot freeze her, inoculated
against time. Today the physio
will come again, the IV tubes
will have their tangling roots untied.
But the god has not drawn back his hand.

Today's egg will turn into tomorrow's bird.
Today's river will reach tomorrow's ocean.

The flight attendant puts down a tray —
food portioned out for us, utensils subtly too small.
It swims in front of me, transmogrified by tears
into metaphor.

I am turning her into a branch of laurel,
Apollo's light-limbed bride.
And I think that this is wrong, all
wrong to turn her into the poem
she must write
herself.

The great work

In antique alchemical texts, stiff woodcuts picture 'the great work' of producing the Philosopher's Stone as a marriage. Sol and Luna (lying in a marriage bed, devoured by the green dragon, then rising again in royal robes) illustrate and disguise the chemical transformations occurring in the alchemist's beakers and retorts.

The primary dictum: solve et coagula — *separate and join together.*

Calcination

The red man to lie down with his white queen
unclothed in the green land of honeymoon,
                its island breadth.

After the patient/impatient months of preparation
and longing, the fierce heats
                of their young breath.

The prank thistle in the bedclothes, the fire
of laughter. Sheep on the hillside like clouds
                of released breath.

The sheep gathering as she teaches him to sing.
'*Mi, fah. Fah.*' '*Bah*,' the sheep sing back to them,
                with their grass breath.

The hot wonder of becoming one.
A rebis creature, fused bodies,
                separate breaths.

Digestion

Hen on egg, warm sun on mud
breed change. Set sunlight to brood
    on a sealed flask.

The child planted so soon,
seed of gold and silver in her womb —
    tight-luted flask.

Poems simmering in his head all day
at the shipyard, held warm like tea
    in his thermos flask.

Their first-born's easy birth, expelled
from the caul's cracked luting, Sunday's child.
    The future's flask.

These early days of delight, nest
of the next five decades, the resin paste
    that seals their flask.

Fermentation

Sugars the substrate — sugars of milk, sugars of grain,
the common stuff of life effervescing
    Yeast's rising play.

Do it again. Do it again, Daddy!
The children squeal and run, giddy
    with bed-time's play

His ever-elaborating stories, the adventures
growing ever more rococo —
    a fountain's play

and the kids peeing themselves with laughter,
returned to 'Wash-Up Land,' exhausted into rest
    at last, by play.

The dough risen and baked, honey elated into mead,
fruit into wine. The cheese curds pressed.
    Nourishment's display.

The white wife smiles at the ferment
she could not make alone, at what he fuels —
    the fire's play.

Fixation

Mercury, metal's bright soul, held in heat
becomes a red lump, an ox-like oxide,
    its restlessness fixed.

What do you want me to be, Mary?
he asks from the set kitchen table, where
    tea has been fixed.

His quicksilver soul longs to be hart on the hills,
to breathe more than smoke in the shipyard
    where his life is fixed.

Her iron's hard nose is sniffing seams and corners
and the round rivets of his overalls. The board-hard cotton
    flattened and fixed.

*If you're going to be a painter, then just you be
a good one*, she says to the wrinkle
    where her gaze is fixed.

He sighs like a pole-yoked ox at the plough's turn.
She is his Pole Star. For better and for worse,
    pole stars are fixed.

Filtration

From the glutinous sludge of putrefaction
the adept must separate the grosser section
    from the subtler part.

The red man ties a piece of his wife's old stocking
tight round the rim of an empty paint can.
    This sieve will part

the thickened scum of aging paint, poured slowly
through its mesh. He prods the shreds and oily
    remnant part.

His life this constant straining. Sordid,
the stockings with their sticky curds discarded,
    set apart.

He takes up the tubes of vivid poison — chromes,
leads, orpiments — needed for the shadings
    their pastes impart

and stirs their colours into silky streams of paint.
He crafts the subtlest tinctures, tints —
    a tired wizard's part —

accepts the toxic fumes ascending steadily.
In the work of providing for a family
    he does his part.

Ceration

*The mollification of an hard thing not fusible
unto liquefaction.* The grinding and combining
    into pliant wax.

For much that is hard in life, there is no solvent,
no alkahest. Only the hope of softening
    its stiff-sealed wax.

Some afternoons, he slips away
from the paint pots, the ladders and rollers
    and the putty's grey wax

to the basement apartment, sweet with toys.
The children at school. The air with the scent
    of her polishing wax.

In that containment, the sweet balm
of bodies. Healing electuary. The honey's comb
    sealed with wax.

And afterwards, tea, dulcet with sugar.
Their voices soft together, in these cupped days
    that wane and wax.

Distillation

Aqua ardens — the water that burns. Afflatus
steaming from the alchemist's apparatus,
    collecting spirit.

Alcohol drips from the retort's glass crescent.
A fluid that can fix fragrances, quintessence —
    the rose's spirit.

Open the vessel. The upper layer is sky-blue,
brings people crowding to the house and birds to windows —
    the sky in high spirits.

Its lower layer lies turbid — Caliban,
quarrelsome demon. A mean
    maligne spirit.

Vitriol, the green dragon with corrosive wings,
eats itself in its glass dungeon — gold-consuming
    nitre's spirit.

The red man unscrews the top of the whisky bottle.
His white wife watches. What will emerge this time
    from his volatile spirit?

Congelation

Dry. The stolid heat that does not burn
but evaporates relentlessly, driving out water.
    The dessicating work.

A thickening syrup in the crucible.
And then the crystals. All that's left from the first
    wearisome work.

The white and hardened plaster of hearts.
The getting up in the morning. All that's shared, now:
    the drive to work.

This is the end of the first stage. The white stone.
All its rainbow colours gone. This hard known,
    on which they work.

Only the stubborn residue of love.
Staying together for the children, to make
    the house work.

Sublimation

Certain solids can become a spirit of themselves, a vapour
that cools to form pure crystals on the roof
    of the alembic's cave.

Translation to a higher form, Christ the Stone
of Philosophers, borne up on warm wings of angels —
    what low matter craves.

He turns the tissue pages of the Bible, to read
a chapter every morning. The red man seeks ascendance
    from his cramped cave.

The grim Old Testament with its clashing nonsense
bemuses his brain. Its battles and begots, caught
    in a black-cowled cave.

And you think you're so holy, sitting there!
His white-lipped wife wipes the table, dishrag flapping
    like a bat in a cave.

He looks up at her from ancient tales of murder
and treachery, starts to laugh, emerges
    from his hermit cave.

It becomes their joking catch-phrase — *Oh, you're so holy.*
A deposition of laughter. Light let down like wings
    in a sunlit cave.

Union through solution

An alloy is metal dissolved in metal.
Gold in silver, silver in gold, becomes electrum —
    brightness united.

Solution and resolution — more than seam or weld.
This is true amalgam, substance
    in substance united.

In fifty years, they have come to look alike.
Always hand in hand, much of a height,
    their steps united.

The leprechauns, they're called, as if they know
gold's hiding place. Affection and a trace of envy
    of hearts so united.

Small and almost magical they seem.
The Red King and his White Queen,
    kingdoms united.

Union through multiplication

Never arrived at — the philosopher's stone.
Yet the magus knew it would be red and brilliant,
    a translucent body.

More lustrous than the windows in cathedrals
glass turned ruby by powder of gold, instilled
    into its liquid body.

Sunset glows ahead of them on the long highway
home to the humdrum — a crimson hem
    to the sky's high body.

Quarrels litter the road behind them
like hubcaps and rusting mufflers lost
    from their old car's body.

Silence makes a hard stone of their day.
But it is not what they are driving towards —
    so incarnadine a body

that it alters hearts. The cold white lady
reaches for his warm hand,
    touch of his body.

The sky is multiplying itself into fire
and the red sun sinks like a lump of cinnabar.
    The transforming body

that they will try and try to reach, driving on
into the proliferating lights the city wears
    on its jangled body.

Past the lesser signage of duty and detour, they take
their changed hearts. Beauty creates love. Love
    wears beauty's body.

Union through projection

To change — that was the dream. To touch
with stone or elixir. Lead burgeoning into gold.
    Souls growing upward.

A home-made kite, cobbled from lumber and string,
plated with newspaper. How could so clumsy a thing
    ever reach skyward?

But the red king carries it to the cliff-edge park
and the white queen in her high heels, laughing,
    gallops forward.

The children, puzzled but happy as puppies,
caper on the chubby legs that soon will lengthen
    to carry them forward.

And for an amazing moment, the kite lifts
its crazy face into the wind
    tugging skyward.

The children touch the kitchen twine, taut,
and feel they hold the sky's own tail,
    its yearning upward.

We have to reach the stars, he always told them,
dreaming the human race perfectible
    and racing outward.

The kite collapses in a nose dive to the grass,
endeavour crumpled. They yelp and laugh and will try again
    to raise it upward.

A line of projection that carries points and angles
to another plane, the touching geometry
    that bears us onward.

Glosa: The Weather

> *This is guesswork, this is love.*
> *This is giving up gorgeousness to please you,*
> *you beautiful dead to be. God bless*
> *the weather and the words. Any words. Any weather.*
>   —John Newlove, 'The Weather'

Why does it matter that you died
in summer? As though the weather
writes in necessary, sympathetic metaphor.
For both of you, I wanted
only the kindliest of seasons.
    As if such linkages would prove
you blessed. Sweet May, July's long day.
Lilac, cirrus, rose, campanula.
    Why this longing for correlative?
    This is guesswork, this is love.

You, mother, on this warm May afternoon,
knees drawn to one side like a child
drowsing in a hammock. A gold light on your skin
as though pollen dusted it. Such a colour
I have never seen. So gilded, beautiful
    while death waits to ease you.
The nurse slips the harsh red circles of her stethoscope
under your lilac gown, tells us what we know.
    We watch the silver of the moon release you,
    giving up gorgeousness to please you.

Death is great work, father. You breathe hard
throughout the short night of July, your fine jaw set,
a man determined to complete a race.
As a child you reached the tape and stopped.
Another boy took your picnic prize.
    This time you will cross.
Dawn melts sky into a copper haze.
Fluid melts from your cells, soaks sheets
    with the determined sweat of changefulness.
    You beautiful dead to be. God bless.

This, your last, great gift — that I may go with you
through the warm white weather,
murmuring our last words. *Love. Remember.
Together.* To hold your hands
while the eyes slide shut.
    To know this is as common as the weather.
To feel, as living symbols, deer on the lawn,
a stream of gulls, hares browsing in the twilight.
    A world charged with meaning. What we have forever —
    the weather and the words. Any words. Any weather.

Acknowledgements

The author thanks the Canada Council for the Arts for financial assistance in completing this manuscript.

A number of the poems from *Eve learns endearments* previously appeared in the anthology "Poetry as Liturgy" from St. Thomas Press.

Deep field experiment won cv2's "Poetics of Space" contest and appeared in that magazine.

Suncatcher was first published in The *Edmonton Journal*.

Glosa: Parting appeared on the Parliamentary Poet Laureate's "Poem of the Week" website (June 2008).

Glosa: The Weather appeared in *The Literary Review of Canada*.

The form of "The Great Work" is inspired by Mimi Khelvati's use of the ghazal in *The Meanest Flower*.

Notes

PAGE 1: Baucis and Philemon refers to the legend in Ovid's *Metamorphoses* about an elderly couple rewarded for their hospitality to the gods by being turned into trees. The epigraph is from the translation by Charles Martin (2004, W.W. Norton & Company, New York).

PAGE 14: "We could not see without our tears." Tom Lutz, *Crying: A Natural and Cultural History of Tears* (1999, W.W. Norton & Company, New York), p. 67.

PAGE 25: The quatrain from Pablo Neruda's poem "La Memoria" is based on the translation by Alisdair Reid. I have altered the final phrase to "yard by yard."

"Mnemosyne's clear spring" — Mnemosyne is goddess of memory and mother of the Muses. She is associated with two sources of water, the spring that holds all memory, and the River Lethe, whose waters induce forgetting. The Pythagorean doctrine of transmigration held that forgetting was a necessary step in the transition to the soul's next life.

PAGE 29: In Scotland, a "burn" is a small stream.

PAGE 30: The Hubble space telescope is being used for "deep field experiments" — photographs that focus on very small regions of the sky to collect light from very distant galaxies, allowing astronomers to gain more knowledge about the past evolution of the universe.

PAGE 39: The furnaces used for cremation are known as "retorts" — a word from alchemy that was adopted by the Industrial Revolution. In an industrial context, it describes a sealed combustion chamber in which the material being heated does not come in contact with the fuel.

PAGE 42: At the Clyde Iron Works in 1828, the invention of the hot blast process transformed the cost of iron production and made Glasgow a centre for iron and steel manufacturing. The puddling furnace transformed pig iron produced in the blast furnaces into steel by burning off carbon and other impurities. Carbon dioxide formed in the process causes the slag to puff up on top.

"Vast columns of light" is a phrase from a satiric poem about Clyde Iron Works, "Colin D'lap," by Alexander Rodger (1784–1846).

PAGE 43: The first demonstration of a cremation chamber capable of disposing of a human body took place at the Vienna exposition in 1873. Sir Henry Thompson was surgeon to Queen Victoria and an early proponent for cremation as "a necessary sanitary precaution against the propagation of disease in a population daily growing larger in relation to the area it occupied."

PAGE 44: The Aberlour orphanage, where my mother was placed after her own mother's death in 1927, had been founded in 1882. The nineteenth century saw a surge in the founding of orphanages to deal with children displaced from families by a variety of social trends, including disease and the social impacts of rapid industrialization in Britain.

PAGE 50: "Ceria's incandescent sparkle" — The Welsbach gas mantle was patented in the 1886, after nearly a century of experimentation in burning coal gas to produce light. A cotton stocking was soaked in a solution of "rare earths" — thorium oxide with a trace of ceria added — then shaped and dried. Fitted around the burning gas jet, the mantle vastly increased the flame's light. The mantle became a huge commercial success and was the basis for household gas lighting throughout the early part of the 20th century.

PAGE 54: "Persistence of vision" refers to the psychological phenomenon that underlies motion pictures. The eye retains a visual image for a fraction of a second after its source has been removed. The zoetrope was developed in the 1830s as a hollow drum with a strip of pictures around its inner surface.

PAGE 57: "Pits and lands" are the bumps and smooth spaces that encode data on a video disc.

PAGE 60: The *Cutty Sark*, one of the last great clipper ships to operate on the Australia-Britain wool run. She was completed in 1869 at William Denny's shipyard in Dumbarton, on the Clyde. She was named for a character in Robert Burns' much-loved poem, "Tam O'shanter" — the comely witch in a short shift who nearly catches Tam on his wild ride. The famous overhauling of the *Britannia* took place in 1889.

PAGE 63: "Noddy" was the main character in a series of books by the children's author, Enid Blyton.

PAGE 65: the "uniformity system" developed by Eli Terry in 1808 is considered the forerunner of the assembly line. Prior to this, clocks were made individually by craftsmen and parts for one clock were not interchangeable with the parts for another.

PAGE 66: The escapement is a device that converts rotational motion (for example an unwinding spring) into discrete "ticks." It is a key part of any mechanical clock.

PAGE 70: Nitrocellulose ("gun cotton") was one of the first "smokeless" explosives discovered. The products of the old "black powder" firearms were more than half solids, and smoke on battlefields was a serious issue for troops.

Cordite was developed late in the nineteenth century and extensively used in armaments in the first and second World Wars. In the manufacturing process, its mixture of nitroglycerin and nitrocellulose was known as The Devil's Porridge.

At the Dalbeattie Cordite Works in Scotland, where my mother worked for a time during the war, "the auld maids in P6" worked in the Block Pressing Room. This was the most fume-laden and dangerous part of the manufacturing process, where only mature women worked.

PAGE 72–73: The area around Glasgow was known as "Red Clydeside" for its long history of political activism. The heavily industrialized region provided much of the materiel — ships, steel, armaments and munitions — for British war efforts, and during the first world war munitions workers were predominantly women. In 1915, spiraling rents and tenant evictions prompted protests by "Mrs. Barbour's Army" — named for main organizer, Mary Barbour. The spreading unrest forced the government to respond with the *Rent Restriction Act*.

Lyddite is an explosive mixture of picric acid and collodion. One of the factories set up to manufacture it during World War I was located in the Argyll Works, in the Vale of Leven, near Dumbarton. "The Admiralty Cottages" housed workers known who were known locally as "the Canaries."

PAGE 76: When a film is exposed to light, tiny clusters of metallic silver atoms form in the layer of halide crystals. "Developing" is necessary to amplify the clusters so the "latent image" on the film can become visible. When photography was invented, one of its most common early uses was for post-mortem photographs of loved ones.

PAGE 85: "Time is how" — this sonnet sequence owes much to Richard Dawkins' book on evolution, *The Ancestor's Tale*.

PAGE 86: The legend of Lycaon, king of Arcadia, is told in Book 1 of Ovid's *Metamorphoses*.

PAGE 88: Adenine and thymine are two of the four bases that make up DNA.

PAGE 83: Mitochondria are the small organelles inside each animal cell that use oxygen to provide energy. They have a separate ring of DNA from the genome in the cell's nucleus, and mitochondrial DNA can be traced back through female ancestry.

PAGE 91: "And who could believe such wonders emerge out of eggshells" comes from Book XV of Ovid's *Metamorphoses*, (line 448 of Charles Martin's translation). In a long soliloquy, Pythagoras lectures about the continual changefulness of life and the doctrine of reincarnation.

PAGE 94: "Red beds" are bands of sedimentary rock. Their red colour comes from the oxidization of iron — an indication that the earth's atmosphere finally contained enough oxygen to permit the reaction when the rocks were forming.

PAGE 96: Waxwings are named for small bead-like tips of bright red on their wing feathers.

PAGE 97: Conodonts are extinct eel-like creatures. The name was originally given to small widely found fossils whose body plan puzzled paleontologists. Only later was it realized that these "bones" were actually tooth-like structures used by creatures that had no other bony structures.

PAGE 111–26: The ghazals of *The Great Work* are structured according to twelve major processes that alchemists used in their attempts to create the Philosopher's Stone. Many of the techniques and discoveries of alchemy became the basis for chemistry. They were based on practical laboratory work that led to consistent, repeatable findings.

The last two, Multiplication and Projection, were never achieved. These were hypothetical processes that would realize the alchemists' ambition of transforming matter into its highest state. Through "multiplication," the alchemist would be able to make the stone itself. Through "projection," he or she would be able to transform other matter by touching it with the stone.

The names of some of the processes are familiar today. The less familiar terms are:
- *Calcination*: the hot, dry roasting of substances in that resulted in a metal forming an oxide (or "earth").

- *Digestion:* applying gentler heat to materials within a sealed vessel.
- *Fixation:* the process of making a volatile substance fixed or solid.
- *Ceration:* making a substance soft and waxy, accomplished by slowly adding liquid and heating.
- *Congelation:* the process by which something congeals or thickens, sometimes to the point of crystallizing.
- *Sublimation:* the transition from solid to gas phase, with no intermediate liquid stage.

Other alchemical terms:
- *The Red Man* or *Red King:* gold (also known as Sol).
- *The White Queen:* silver, the moon (also known as Luna).
- *Rebis:* a hermaphroditic figure in alchemical illustrations, that joined Sol and Luna.
- *Luting:* the practice of sealing a flask with a resinous paste (or "lute") that produces an airtight seal.
- *Orpiment* and *realgars*: arsenic-bearing minerals, highly poisonous but used as a pigment for their bright yellow colour.
- *Alkahest:* a hypothetical "universal solvent" capable of dissolving any substance.